With thanks to Antoine and Jean-Jacques Terrasse, Claire Frèches, Céline Julhiet, Claire Blandin, and Anne de Margerie.

All of the illustrations in this book are reproductions of works by Pierre Bonnard (paintings, drawings, lithographs) except for the painting reproduced on page 33, *The Talisman,* which is by Paul Sérusier.

Graphics and layout by Thomas Gravemaker, X-Act
© Éditions de la Réunion des musées nationaux, 1993
49, rue Etienne Marcel, 75001 Paris
© Spadem, Adagp, 1993
English translation © Peter Bedrick Books, 1997

Library of Congress Cataloging-in-Publication Data
    Sellier, Marie.
    [B comme Bonnard. English]
    Bonnard from A to Z / Marie Sellier.
    p.   cm.
    ISBN 0-87226-479-3
    1. Bonnard, Pierre, 1867-1947—Dictionaries.
    I. Bonnard, Pierre, 1867-1947. II. Title.
    N6853.B57S4513 1997
    760'.092—dc21   97-28046
                                                                CIP

Printed in Mexico
First American edition 1997

Bonnard
from A to Z

Marie Sellier

Translated from the French by
Claudia Zoe Bedrick

For Julien, Baptiste, Pierre, and Dora

PETER BEDRICK BOOKS
NEW YORK

Contents

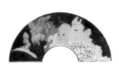

Pierre Bonnard is born on October 3, 1867. Many years later, he will depict himself as a chubby baby on his grandmother's knee.

Avocat

Lawyer

January, 1887. It is extremely cold in the Law School. To warm himself, the professor, sporting an unruly mustache, paces back and forth while he lectures. In the fourth row, a thin, serious student takes notes. He is 20 years old and his name is Pierre — Pierre Bonnard. Like most of his fellow students, he is preparing for a career in law.

While he is a good student, he applies himself only when he wishes to do so. If today one were to look back into his class notebooks, more drawings than

Pierre is 20 when he paints this landscape.

notes would be found. From those sketches, it is evident that Pierre knows how to draw. And he loves to.

This, however, is not a secret to anyone. While still at the Law School, he enrolls at the Academy Julian, a painting school which prepares students for the School of Fine Arts.

Bulles

Bubbles

Sparkling champagne bubbles mark Pierre's official entry into the art world. Having passed the bar exam, he is poised to become a lawyer, when suddenly the label France-Champagne buys his design for a poster for one hundred francs. In 1891, one hundred francs is a small fortune.

On hearing the news, his father, Eugène Bonnard, dances for joy in the garden of the family house.

Having spent his life as a civil servant in the Ministry of War, he is delighted to have a son who is a painter.

Plastered throughout the streets of Paris, Pierre's poster draws much attention.

The painter Henri de Toulouse-Lautrec likes it so much that he hangs it on the wall of his own studio.

Pierre's poster is an event in the history of advertising.

FRANCE CHAMPAGNE

E. DEBRAY
PROPRIÉTAIRE

LA HAUBETTE-TINQUEUX-LEZ-REIMS

BUREAU DE REPRÉSENTATIONS
8, RUE DE L'ISLY PARIS

Chiens et chats

Dogs and Cats

It is summer, 1890. Pierre has just arrived at the family home in Grand-Lemps, in the small village of Dauphiné. Each summer, the Bonnards spend their vacation there. His parents, Eugène and Elise, and his grandmother, Grandma Mertzdorff, welcome him. There he finds Charles, his older brother, Andrée, his younger sister, and all of his four-legged friends, which include the large spaniels, Ravagean and Bella, Fachol, the basset hound, and many old farm dogs. As for the cats, they live gracefully and easily, as cats tend to do. One stretches in the sun while the other lies in wait for the mother duck's downy ducklings.

Pierre narrows his eyes and observes.

Pierre paints two poodles rolling in the grass.

DO RE MI FA SOL LA SI DO RE MI FA SOL LA

Do, mi, sol, do...
This is Claude. With a
great burst of laughter, he
plays a majestic chord.
Claude Terrasse is a
composer. He marries
Pierre's sister, Andrée,
when she is only 17.
Pierre gets along very
well with his energetic

Vu par Pierre,
Claude Terrasse,
son beau-frère.

Claude Terrasse, his
brother-in-law, as
seen by Pierre.

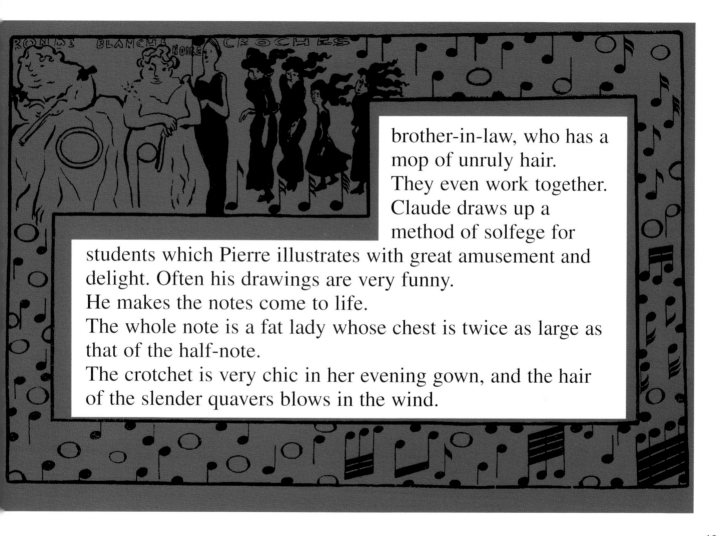

brother-in-law, who has a mop of unruly hair.
They even work together. Claude draws up a method of solfege for students which Pierre illustrates with great amusement and delight. Often his drawings are very funny.
He makes the notes come to life.
The whole note is a fat lady whose chest is twice as large as that of the half-note.
The crotchet is very chic in her evening gown, and the hair of the slender quavers blows in the wind.

Esquisse

Sketch

In the morning, Pierre likes to disappear before breakfast to take a solitary walk.
In his pocket, he carries a sketch book.
He sees, breathes, and seizes in rapid strokes the life which pulsates around him.
He gathers images and smells.
His pencil sketches are light. Several lines, nothing more.

In Pierre's sketch books, children and farm animals play happily together.

14

In Grand-Lemps, he draws little rabbits with their noses in the air, and the chickens and roosters who go about in the farm yard.
In Paris, he sketches the fleeting silhouettes of passersby: a young woman crossing the street, children hurrying in the rain.
From sketch to sketch, Pierre collects the pieces of life which will animate his paintings.

Hurry, hurry, to school!

The basket of this little laundress is very heavy.

PAPA MAMAN BÉBÉ

Famille

Family

The family circle grows. In the home of Andrée and Claude Terrasse, babies follow one upon the other. Six in seven years! Jean, Charles, Renée, Robert, Marcel, Vivette… four boys and two girls. Pierre, Uncle Pierre,

Summer 1898. Andrée, Renée, Robert and an acrobatic cat.

is crazy about his nephews and nieces. In the summer at Grand-Lemps, he photographs and sketches them.

The children play in the garden, scruffy and happy. When it is hot, they splash in the pool in front of the house. Grandma Mertzdorff, imposing in her black dress, watches over her brood. Elise Bonnard takes care of things in the kitchen.

Andrée, in spite of her pregnancies, retains an air of adolescence. Since the beginning, she has been her brother's favorite model.

At the Bonnards', family history is told through paintings.

The Terrasse family in 1900.

Gourmandise

Appetite

An image of appetite:
Black, the big black dog, devours a cherry tart with his eyes.
The table has pride of place in Pierre's paintings, graciously set, it invites the family to eat.
"To the table," calls Elise Bonnard.
The children bounce into the dining room with grubby hands and eyes sparkling. Large white napkins are tied around the children's necks.
A light colored soup is already steaming in their plates.
The cat rubs itself easily against the feet of a chair. It knows that soon it will be able to leap

Little Charles' lunch.

The meal is not over for everyone!

onto the table to finish an abandoned chop. It is not by chance that the poet, Guillaume Apollinaire, compared Bonnard's painting to a "greedy little girl." His paintings give one appetite.

Hiver

Winter

As much as the paintings of Grand-Lemps have the flavor of vacation and late summer, those of the Paris streets suggest winter.

From the studio which he shares with Edouard Vuillard, his friend and fellow painter, Pierre observes the street.

The elegant gentlemen wear top-hats, the women have graceful figures, and the children on their way to school resemble elves in their large capes. A bus passes. A young woman opens her umbrella.

Le pont des Arts in Paris, 1898.

It begins to rain, and Pierre delights in seeing the outline of things become more vivid.

He likes to isolate the small, amusing detail, a gesture or an attitude, typical or unusual. Beginning with his sketches from life, he will compose twelve lithographs which he will publish in 1898, entitled, *Several Aspects of Life in Paris*.

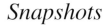

Instantanés

Snapshots

When Pierre discovers photography around 1890, hand-held cameras are just beginning to appear.
This is good news for amateurs. These small, magical cameras enchant the painter. He plays at being a reporter, thrilled at being able to contain so many living images within

that mysterious black box.
A cat jumps into a thicket.
How funny Grandma Mertzdorff looks in her large sun
hat and shawl. Little Renée pets her dog.
The children splash in the pool along with their parents.
These photos are each different yet similar, as family
photos tend to be.
The camera becomes a second sketch book.

In 1894, Pierre designs this poster for *La Revue blanche.*

Journaliste

Journalist

Properly speaking, it is not a newspaper but a review. And what a review! For more than a decade, from 1889 to 1903, *La Revue blanche* will include among its "journalists" the greatest writers, poets and painters of the period. From its earliest beginnings, Pierre is a most faithful collaborator, as are Henri de Toulouse-Lautrec, Edouard Vuillard, Felix Vallotton, Maurice Denis and many other painters. For all of them, participating in *La Revue blanche* is a great adventure of art and friendship. Ties with the Natanson Brothers who run the *Revue* are strong, especially with Thadée who is the editor-in-chief. Like the others, Pierre is charmed by Thadée's wife, the beautiful Misia Natanson. Nothing in the world would keep him from their parties, many in Paris and at their country house in the summer.

Misia arrives in the office of *Le Revue blanche.*

Kakémono

In the spring of 1890, Pierre is seized by the Japanese craze. At the School of Fine Arts, there is a large exhibition of Japanese engravings which includes some exceptionally beautiful kakemonos, the vertical Japanese scroll paintings done on silk or paper.

Pierre paints these *Women in the Garden* in 1891.

The compositions are simple and the motifs decorative, with bright colors taking the place of perspective.
Pierre is overwhelmed. He cuts his canvas to the dimensions of the kakemonos and paints in a Japanese style. He covers the walls of his room with cheap Japanese reproductions which he finds by chance at some of the large department stores.

Although his painter friends in the Nabi group share his attraction to Japanese art, they still are amused by his tremendous enthusiasm and nickname him "the very Japanese Nabi."

Again it is Andrée who poses for this *Woman and Cat*.

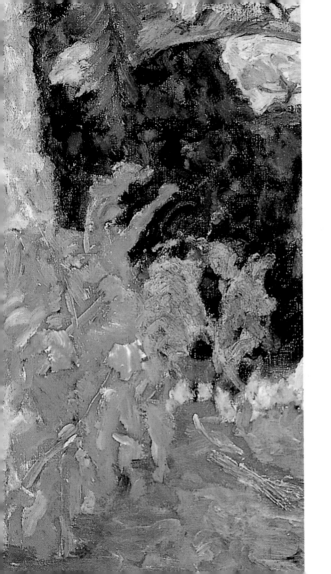

Lauriers-roses

Rose Laurel

In 1909, Pierre writes to his mother: "I have been swept away as by *The Thousand-and-One Nights.*" His great enthusiasm arises from his discovery of the South.
In St. Tropez, which was then only a modest and charming fishing port, he penetrates into a paradise of rose laurel, mimosas, lavender and fragrant thyme.
The colors are glorious. There are wonderful yellows, blues and

In the South, Pierre discovers the light which enlivens his colors.

a rich rose-orange. Even the grays are bursting with light. Pierre does not forget the deep and lasting impression which the South makes on him when he is twenty-two. Several years later, in 1925, he buys a rose-colored house in Cannet, called "Le Bosquet." It is there that he will choose to live at the end of his life.

1912 — late afternoon in St. Tropez.

Marthe

Although her real name is Maria, Maria Boursin, she prefers to be called Marthe.

Pierre meets her in 1893 by sheer chance when he helps her to cross a street.

Marthe is twenty-four years old when they meet.

She works in a boutique selling artificial flowers.

As part of her work, she strings tiny pearls onto metal wires. She is slender, has shapely legs, blue eyes, and a husky voice.

Marthe does not yet know that by entering into Pierre's life

she will penetrate to the heart of his work.

Henceforth, she will be his only model.

His key character or figure, Marthe does not pose, or only rarely.

She lives at Pierre's side, and he watches her live.

A round face under a golden cascade: it is Marthe in 1896.

Nabis

Nabi is a Hebrew word which means prophet. It also is the name which a group of twelve painters and sculptors give themselves around 1890. Pierre is part of this group as is his dear friend, Edouard Vuillard.

Roussel, Vuillard and Bonnard in Paris.

Other members include Maurice Denis, Ker-Xavier Roussel, Paul Sérusier, and Félix Vallotton. All of them knew each other at school and shared an admiration for one of their elders, the painter Paul Gauguin.

The Nabis have their treasure. It is a highly colored landscape which Paul Serusier painted on a small panel of wood under Gauguin's guidance. It is known as *The Talisman*. Despite that magical element, however, the group is nothing like a secret society.

Their main idea is that everything should be a work of art: a plate and a wardrobe as much as a painting or a sculpture.

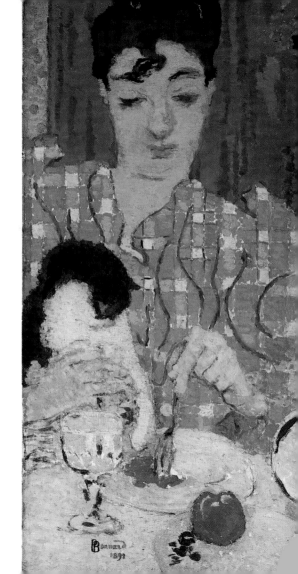

A masterpiece of the Nabi period: Andrée and her cat.

Claude, Andrée, and Jean, their son.

Women, flowers, dogs, and a cat appear in the design for a fan.

Objets

Objects

Aptly called "the very Japanese Nabi," Pierre is passionate about the objects, especially the screens and fans, which the French have borrowed from the Japanese.

He designs screens which resemble nothing yet seen. There too, he depicts his delicate and light-hearted world, where women are mothers, children play, and little dogs wag their tails. Likewise, on the charming curve of a fan, we encounter the surprised face of a baby who is none other than his nephew, Jean.

Rolling hoops.

Pierre seizes upon everything. He designs plates and pots, sideboards and dressers. His exploration is a great creative celebration.

He paints dogs, one of his usual images, on the door of a sideboard.

Petit monde

Marthe feeds the cat, as she does everyday.

Small World

"A painting," says Pierre, "is a small world which one makes for oneself." In order for this little world to remain standing, its construction must be solid. Imagination does not suffice. Pierre is well aware of that, however, and it is not that which he depicts. Everything in his paintings is simple. There is a lightness and charm which resembles improvisation, but chance plays little role. Pierre works rigorously, reflecting upon and retouching his work. In great art, however, the labor which goes into a work cannot be seen. The little world to which Pierre compares painting is the image of his own contained world, the one in which he lives with Marthe. It is a protected and harmonious world, a cocoon-world, sheltered from the larger, real world in which, at this time, men are fighting each other and countries are at war.

A white interior of 1929: a small, luminous world.

Queues-de-cerises

Cherry Stems

Cherry stems are the little nothings of everyday which, placed end to end, make up a life: a breakfast which lasts forever, a bouquet bursting forth from a vase, or a plateful of cherries. In short, nothing very extraordinary.

Some fruit…

Pierre has no taste for the sensational. He paints what he sees around him as well as self-portraits. Pierre lives through two world wars and continues to paint Marthe, his dog, and flowers.

At the height of the conflicts, he remains unperturbed, noting the weather in his diary day after day: "beautiful," "cloudy," "rainy." Weather, in order to forget the cannons.

…some flowers, that is all.

Roulotte

Pierre has three homes: a studio in Paris, a pink house in Cannet, and another at Vernonnet in the Eure.
The latter is called Ma Roulotte.
It's a simple house with a beautiful wooden balcony overlooking the Seine.
At Vernonnet, the surroundings are green, the light dramatic and the tugboats passing

A view from the terrace of Ma Roulotte.

on the Seine sparkle on the water.

From there, Pierre goes next door to visit his neighbor, an old man with a bushy beard who lives at Giverny. His name is Claude Monet.

Although Pierre loves the warm, enveloping light of the South, he cannot dispense with the North because, as he says, "the light in the South changes all the time."

Pierre's canvases play a part in this. Rolled on the roof of his car, they accompany him through all his travels.

Pierre and Marthe on the balcony.

Pierre et Claude Monet at Giverny around 1925.

Salle de bains

The Bath

Marthe does not feel well. Her health, which has always been fragile begins to decline.

She becomes gloomy and anxious. The only place where she feels well is in the bath. The water calms her. Stretched out in the bath, she dreams and escapes.

Pierre follows her and, in a quick sketch, captures the brilliancy of the water and the play of light over the checkered floor. Under his brush, the common linoleum becomes a golden mosaic, shadows glow and Marthe's body shines like mother of pearl.

When he paints Marthe in the bath, Pierre becomes a magician.

In the bathroom, Marthe becomes almost aerial.

1943: Landscape of the Côte d'Azur.

Pierre uses a plate
as a palette.

Taches *Daubs*

To watch Pierre at work, it is necessary to follow him into his studio where he paints.

Pierre never paints out-of-doors, which is to say, from nature. His sketches are his starting point. They translate his first impression.

He recreates color from memory.

Since he does not like to be limited by a frame, Pierre works on white canvas pinned to the wall.

With his paintbrush in one hand and a cloth in the other, he paints with small daubs, standing very near to the canvas. To judge his work, he takes a step back, and puts his hand over his eyes to shade them from the light.

According to Bonnard, "A painting is a series of daubs, which when linked to one another, end up forming an object."

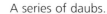

A series of daubs.

Ubu

Ubu as an aviator.

Father Ubu is an odd character. He is shaped like a pear, has an imposing nose, and three mustache hairs. His expressions are as gross as he is. At every turn, he bellows "Sausagehead," "By my green snot!" and hurls a thundering "Squwadge!" This impossible character is invented around 1888 by Alfred Jarry, a friend of Claude Terrasse's. It is Claude who writes the

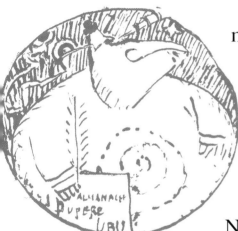

A drawing
for the cover of the
Almanac of 1901.

music to *King Ubu* and who,
along with Jarry, creates the
Pantins Puppet Theater.
Claude installs the theater in his
apartment, welcoming their
performances.
The marionettes and the settings are
created by Pierre and his friends.
Next, Pierre amuses himself by designing
Father Ubu's two almanacs and his bizarrely
comic calendar where St. Hair lives happily with
St. Soup. In the land of Ubu, nothing is sacred.
In tribute to the laughter which he shares with
Jarry, Pierre calls his basset hound, Ubu.

The dog, Ubu.

47

Vibrations

Self-Portrait of 1945.

The sweet and gentle Pierre who never raises his voice paints with surprising force, even violently.
He uses colors at maximum strength, and dares unexpected combinations which give the impression that his paintings almost exist in the realm of sound.

Just before noon, colors
vibrate in full light.

Reds rub against plums and
pinks, yellows explode on the
canvas, and violet and orange
blend into rust-colored arms.
In their juxtapositions, the
colors confront and electrify
one another.
In Pierre's painting, color is
primary. Even shadows take
on color, becoming red or
burgundy.
There is no gray in Pierre's
world. Color pervades
everything.

Winterthur

The Hahnloser family in a boat.

Hedy Hahnloser

What's the connection between Bonnard and Winterthur?
The small Swiss city near Zurich is where the Hahnlosers live, devoted friends and art connoisseurs.
Pierre meets them around 1916 through Felix Vallotton, the Swiss Nabi.
A respectful friendship links them for over thirty years. Arthur and Hedy Hahnloser visit Pierre regularly and purchase his paintings.
Pierre reserves first choice for them.

Pierre retouches this canvas many times over the seven years before he agrees to sell it to the Hahnlosers.

Arthur Hahnloser.

In 1930, Pierre gets sick and is hospitalized. Arthur Hahnloser suggests that he paint and brings him a lovely box of watercolors. Pierre, however, is so accustomed to painting in oils that the result is disappointing. Hahnloser then brings him tubes of gouache and with them, Pierre creates marvels.

A page from Pierre's diary. Marthe dies on January 26, 1942.

Faithful to Marthe, through love or indifference,
Pierre crosses out the world.
He isolates himself and works. Marthe can no longer
endure any presence other than Pierre's.

She hides herself away in the
house, passing like a shadow from
her room to the bathroom.
   Pierre continues to paint her as
   his heart sees her, which is to say
   as eternally young. And yet,
   Marthe is already nearly 70.
      On January 26, 1942, Pierre, as
      he does every day, notes the
      weather in his diary.
         The day is beautiful. Below
         that entry, he puts a cross, a
         very small cross.
Marthe has died.
To his friend Henri Matisse, he writes:
"My poor Marthe has died from a
heart-attack."
That is all he says. Then he locks the
door to her room.

Yeux bridés

Narrowed Eyes

Lost in an oversized jacket,
wearing a canvas hat, with
narrowed eyes—as he ages, Pierre
looks truly Japanese.
Behind his round glasses, his
myopic eyes are vaguely
melancholic.
He has retained that far-away look
that he already had before he was
twenty. Though he is nearly 80, he
is not taken to be old.
Little by little, his friends die:
Claude Terrasse, Edouard Vuillard,

his brother Charles.
Having painted what was closest to him throughout his life, he now looks into the distance. He paints large landscapes.
At the same time, on the walls of his atelier, he sticks beautiful candy wrappers side-by-side, as in the past when he put up Japanese prints from department stores.

At 78, he paints his reflection in the bathroom mirror.

Zéphyr

His last canvas, his last brush-stroke, a flowering almond tree.

Zephyr

The beautiful almond tree blooms into white flowers. The breeze is so light that it is not wind but a zephyr. On this spring morning in 1946, Pierre's brush is as light as air. Little by little, the outline of a tree takes shape on his canvas. The almond tree emerges in all of its springtime fullness. Never has it looked so beautiful. Does Pierre sense that it is his last spring? In October, he enters his 80th year. His energy begins to

wane. Though weak, he still has the strength to note that an area at the bottom of the canvas displeases him.

He asks his nephew Charles to guide his hand so that he might add a touch of gold at the root of the tree.

When he dies, several days later on January 23, 1947, the snowflakes drifting down are as light as the petals of the almond tree's flowers.

Fin.

List of Illustrations

Correspondances, 1944. Painting, 1919, Art Museum, Winterthur. Painting, 1896, private collection.

Pages 32-33: Painting, 1892, Musée d'Orsay, Paris. Photo from the R.M.N. Ink Drawing, 1910, private collection. Painting by Paul Sérusier, 1888, Musée d'Orsay, Paris. Photo from the R.M.N. Painting, 1892, Musée d'Orsay, Paris. Photo from the R.M.N.

Pages 34-35: Plan for a fan, watercolor, 1891, private collection. Plan for a fan, oil, 1892, private collection. A painted screen, 1897, Musée d'Orsay, Paris. Photo from the R.M.N. Plan for furniture design, watercolor (detail), 1891, Musée du Louvre, Department of Graphic Arts. Photo from the R.M.N.

Pages 36-37: Painting, 1929, Musée de Grenoble, Grenoble. Photo from the Musée de Grenoble.

Pages 38-39: Diary pages from 1934-37, National Library, Paris. Painting, 1923, private collection. Pencil drawing, 1930, private collection. Painting, 1925, Musée Albert-André, Bagnols-sur-Cèze. Photo from Daspet.

Pages 40-41: Painting, 1928, Kunstsammlung Nordrhein Westfalen. Photo by Lauros-Giraudon. Photograph of Pierre and Marthe, 1920, private collection. Photograph of Bonnard and Monet, around 1925, private collection. Drawing from, *The 628 E-8* by O. Mirbeau, 1903.

Pages 42-43: Painting, Musée du Petit Palais, Paris. Photo from the Photographic Department of the Musées de la Ville de Paris. Ink drawing, private collection. Painting, 1914-15, private collection.

Pages 44-45: Detail of a photograph by Henri Cartier-Bresson, 1945. © Henri Cartier-Bresson, Magnum Agency.

Painting, 1945, private collection. Plate-palette by Pierre Bonnard, private collection.

Pages 46-47: Drawing for the *Little Almanac of Father Ubu,* 1899. Illustration for *Father Ubu in the Airfield,* 1918. Cover for the *Illustrated Almanac of Father Ubu,* 1901, National Library, Paris. Pencil drawing, 1913, private collection.

Pages 48-49: Painting, 1930, Musée du Petit Palais, Paris. Photo from the Photographic Department of the Musées de la Ville de Paris. Painting (detail), 1939-45, private collection. Painting, 1946, private collection.

Pages 50-51: Painting, 1924-25, private collection. Photo by Lauros-Giraudon. Pencil sketches, 1923, private collection. Painting, 1928-34, private collection.

Pages 52-53: Pencil drawing, 1938, private collection. Diary page, 1942, National Library, Paris. Painting, 1925, private collection.

Pages 54-55: Photo, 1945, André Ostier. Painting, 1945, private collection. Photo by Beatrice Hatala, Centre G. Pompidou.

Pages 56-57: Photo by André Ostier. Painting, 1947, Musée National d'Art Moderne, Centre Georges Pompidou. Photo from the Centre G. Pompidou. Illustration from *Notes on Love* by C. Anet, 1922.

Page 59: Illustration from *Natural Histories* by Jules Renard, 1904.